Hope's Journey

Betsy Chutchian

Classic Blocks, Reproduction Quilts,
and Stories of Bygone Days

Hope's Journey:
Classic Blocks, Reproduction Quilts, and Stories of Bygone Days
© 2018 by Betsy Chutchian

Martingale®
19021 120th Ave. NE, Ste. 102
Bothell, WA 98011-9511 USA
ShopMartingale.com

Printed in China
23 22 21 20 19 18   8 7 6 5 4 3 2 1

Library of Congress Cataloging-in-Publication Data is available upon request.

ISBN: 978-1-60468-961-7

MISSION STATEMENT

We empower makers who use fabric and yarn to make life more enjoyable.

CREDITS

**PUBLISHER AND
CHIEF VISIONARY OFFICER**
Jennifer Erbe Keltner

CONTENT DIRECTOR
Karen Costello Soltys

MANAGING EDITOR
Tina Cook

ACQUISITIONS EDITOR
Karen M. Burns

TECHNICAL EDITOR
Ellen Pahl

COPY EDITOR
Melissa Bryan

DESIGN MANAGER
Adrienne Smitke

**COVER AND
INTERIOR DESIGNER**
Regina Girard

LOCATION PHOTOGRAPHER
Adam Albright

STUDIO PHOTOGRAPHER
Brent Kane

ILLUSTRATOR
Lisa Lauch

SPECIAL THANKS
*Photography for this book was taken at the home of
Lance and Jodi Allen of Woodinville, Washington,
and at The Garden Barn in Indianola, Iowa.*

Contents

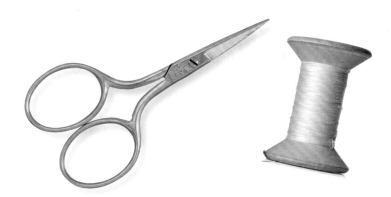

Hope, to me, is the name of every woman and girl who left her home to embark on a journey of uncertain outcome.

Introduction

Hope, to me, is the name of every woman and girl from long ago who left her home to embark on a journey of uncertain outcome. Wives, mothers, daughters, and sisters left the lives they knew and stepped forward into the unknown, either with family or alone, in search of a better life. Whether leaving their home country in search of religious freedom or to escape unfair laws or famine, families and individuals sought refuge in the New World.

As the population grew and settlements increased, families moved west again and again. The frontier advanced in all directions, and opportunities arose. The concept of Manifest Destiny encouraged settlement in the West in an effort to expand US territories and influence. The idea of going west, either to escape crowded cities and poor soil or as a new start with better land and opportunities, enticed men to leave their homes. Women and children had no choice but to go with them. From the 1830s through the 1860s, an estimated 350,000 men, women, and children made the journey westward. Many failed to realize their dreams, while others endured extreme hardships during the overland journey but eventually reached their destination.

I imagine many of these pioneer women had dreams of hope and perseverance. Hope's journey was a mystery. She didn't know what life would be like when she arrived at her destination—nor did she know what to expect from the journey itself. But she went anyway. That is the essence of hope.

The material in this book was originally a yearlong mystery class that I taught as a monthly club. Much like the pioneers' journey, students had no idea where they were going or what the journey would be like. Each month, students received block instructions for a sampler quilt, a pattern for a mini-quilt, and a history lesson pertinent to a pioneer woman's story. Students were encouraged to select a wide variety of fabrics in a palette they loved and to keep a notebook of fabric swatches, notes, quotes, and anything else that might make their journey interesting.

But having this book in front of you eliminates the unknown. Here, each chapter is presented as a monthly lesson, complete with block instructions for the sampler quilt on page 92, history tidbits, and words of encouragement.

Pack your baskets for the journey with a wide variety of prints in a palette you love, in quantities including fat quarters, fat eighths, or yardage and small pieces. I used my own fabric lines and other reproduction fabrics to make the blocks and quilts, but Hope's Journey will look great in any fabric style. The fabrics listed with each block and small quilt are generous so that you can repeat fabrics along the way. You may also want to add more fabrics throughout the journey.

I suggest you cut and save a 2½" square from each and every fabric used in the projects, and then sew them into a charm quilt (page 91). Also save all scraps and leftover units from the blocks to use in the setting of your sampler quilt. You may wish to make more than one of the smaller blocks, depending on the setting you choose for your sampler quilt. You'll find four sampler setting options starting on page 92, and another one online at ShopMartingale.com/HopesJourney. When setting the quilt, you'll add filler blocks and pieces to make Hope's Journey your journey, your quilt.

Just as there are many routes to a final destination, there can be many ways to piece various blocks and units, plus numerous options you can include in the setting. Various techniques and alternatives are presented within the chapters. Be sure to read all the instructions before beginning the blocks or quilts.

I sincerely hope that you join me on this journey and enjoy it every step of the way.

~ *Betsy* ~

CHAPTER 1

Setting Sail

*Hope is an adventure,
a going forward, a
confident search for
a rewarding life.*

~Dr. Karl Menninger

Setting sail for America from England on September 6, 1620, the Mayflower *took 66 days to reach Cape Cod, Massachusetts, not the intended destination of Virginia. Of the 102 passengers aboard this renowned ship, only about half would survive the first winter in the new country.*

While that's most certainly not what the Pilgrims envisioned, what did they think the New World would offer? Could they imagine how incredibly cramped and sickly their quarters on the ship would be? Had they known, would they have set sail regardless?

It's recorded that Dorothy May, wife of the Plymouth Colony's leader, William Bradford, survived the voyage only to slip into the harbor and drown while her husband was on shore. Despairing over leaving their young son back in Europe, did she fall—or jump? Did hopelessness and fear of the unknown overcome her?

In the years that followed, many more ships would arrive, filled with those who left home in search of a better life but were uncertain of what they would face.

Lady of the Lake

10" BLOCK

MATERIALS

Fat quarters are 18" × 21" and fat eighths are 9" × 21".

1 fat eighth of navy floral
1 fat eighth of tan floral
1 fat eighth of navy print
1 fat quarter of tan print

CUTTING

Save all leftover pieces and cut a 2½" square from each fabric to use in Journey's End (page 91).

From the navy floral, cut:
1 square, 7" × 7"; cut in half diagonally to make
    2 triangles (1 is extra)
4 squares, 3" × 3"

From the tan floral, cut:
1 square, 7" × 7"; cut in half diagonally to make
    2 triangles (1 is extra)

From the navy print, cut:
4 squares, 3" × 3"

From the tan print, cut:
8 squares, 3" × 3"

ASSEMBLING THE BLOCK

Press all seam allowances as indicated by the arrows in the illustrations.

1. Sew together a navy floral triangle and a tan floral triangle. Trim the half-square-triangle unit to 6½" square.

 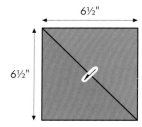

6½"

6½"

Make 1 unit.

2. Draw a diagonal line from corner to corner on the wrong side of each tan print 3" square. Pair a marked square with a navy floral or print 3" square, right sides together. Sew ¼" from each side of the line. Cut on the marked line and press. Make a total of 16 half-square-triangle units. Trim each unit to 2½" square.

2½"

2½"

Make 16 units.

Pressing Pointer

I suggest pressing fabrics with Best Press or your favorite spray starch before cutting. This adds body to improve cutting accuracy and reduces distortion when pressing.

Broken Dishes

6" BLOCK

MATERIALS

2 squares, 8" × 8", of different light prints
1 square, 8" × 8", of brown print
1 square, 8" × 8", of green print

CUTTING

Save all leftover pieces and cut a 2½" square from each fabric to use in Journey's End (page 91).

From *each* light print, cut:
4 squares, 2½" × 2½" (8 total)

From the brown print, cut:
4 squares, 2½" × 2½"

From the green print, cut:
4 squares, 2½" × 2½"

ASSEMBLING THE BLOCK

Press all seam allowances as indicated by the arrows in the illustrations.

1. Draw a diagonal line from corner to corner on the wrong side of four matching light 2½" squares. Pair a marked square with a green 2½" square, right sides together. Sew ¼" from each side of the line. Cut on the marked line and press. Make a total of eight green/light half-square-triangle units. Trim each unit to 2" square. Repeat with the second light print and the brown print to make eight units.

  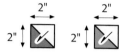

Make 8 of each unit.

2. Sew two of each unit together to make a quarter block that measures 3½" square, including seam allowances. Make four quarter blocks.

Make 4 units,
3½" × 3½".

3. Sew the quarter blocks together as shown to complete the block. It should measure 6½" square, including seam allowances. ✐

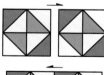 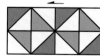 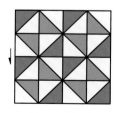

Make 1 block,
6½" × 6½".

Spring Meadow

18½" × 15½" QUILT

Finished blocks: 3" × 3"

Dip into your scraps of pink and green and stitch up half-square-triangle units to welcome spring and remember the women who made the journey across the prairies on their way to a new life.

MATERIALS

Yardage is based on 42"-wide fabric.

⅜ yard *total* of assorted pink prints for blocks*
⅜ yard *total* of assorted green prints for blocks
⅛ yard of pink print for binding
⅝ yard of fabric for backing
20" × 23" piece of batting
1½" finished half-square-triangle papers (optional)

In the quilt shown, these include pink prints on a white or cream background.

CUTTING

Save all leftover pieces and cut a 2½" square from each fabric to use in Journey's End (page 91).

From the assorted pink prints, cut:
12 pairs of matching squares, 2½" × 2½" (24 total)*
9 squares, 4" × 4"

From the assorted green prints, cut:
24 squares, 2½" × 2½"*
9 squares, 4" × 4"

From the pink print for binding, cut:
2 strips, 1⅛" × 42"

Or follow the cutting instructions for the 1½" triangle papers if you're using them.

ASSEMBLING THE BLOCKS

Press all seam allowances as indicated by the arrows in the illustrations.

1. Draw a diagonal line from corner to corner on the wrong side of each pink 2½" square. Pair a marked square with a green 2½" square, right sides together. Sew ¼" from each side of the line. Cut on the marked line and press. Make a total of 48 half-square-triangle units. Trim each block to 2" square.

Make 48 units.

2. Repeat step 1 with the pink and green 4" squares. Make 18 Half-Square Triangle blocks and trim them to 3½" square.

Make 18 blocks.

3. Sew the 2" units together in groups of four. Remove the stitches in the center of the four-patch unit so that you can press the horizontal seam allowances in opposite directions. Make 12 Four Patch blocks that measure 3½" square.

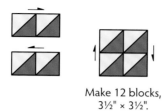

Make 12 blocks,
3½" × 3½".

ASSEMBLING THE QUILT TOP

1. Sew the Four Patch blocks together in three rows of four blocks. Sew the rows together.

2. Sew three of the Half-Square Triangle blocks together to make a side border. Make two. Sew six of the blocks together to make the top border, and repeat to make the bottom border.

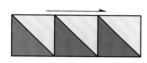

Make 2 side borders,
3½" × 9½".

Make 2 top/bottom borders,
3½" × 18½".

3. Sew the side borders to the quilt center. Sew the top and bottom borders to the quilt center. The quilt top should measure 18½" × 15½".

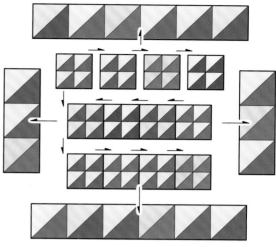

Quilt assembly

FINISHING

For detailed information about any finishing steps, visit ShopMartingale.com/HowtoQuilt.

1. Layer the quilt top, batting, and backing; baste the layers together.

2. Quilt as desired. The quilt shown was quilted in the ditch.

3. Trim the batting and backing even with the quilt top.

4. Using the pink print 1⅛" strips, make and attach single-fold binding. ✿

CHAPTER 3

Prairie Fowl

Chick, Chick, Chick, Hen

15½" × 15½" QUILT

Finished block: 4" × 4"

The block used in this quilt has a number of names, most having something to do with our feathered friends—Wild Goose Chase, Ducklings, Fox and Geese, Duck and Ducklings, and of course, Hen and Chickens.

MATERIALS

Yardage is based on 42"-wide fabric; fat quarters are 18" × 21"; and fat eighths are 9" × 21".

4 fat eighths of assorted cream prints for blocks
4 fat eighths of assorted gold prints for blocks and pieced border
1 fat quarter of blue ombré for setting triangles and binding
1 fat eighth of blue print #1 for sashing and pieced border
1 fat eighth of blue print #2 for pieced border
⅝ yard of fabric for backing
20" × 20" piece of batting
1" finished half-square-triangle papers (optional)

CUTTING

Save all leftover pieces and cut a 2½" square from each fabric to use in Journey's End (page 91).

From *each* cream print, cut:
2 squares, 1¾" × 1¾" (8 total)
4 squares, 1⅝" × 1⅝"; cut in half diagonally to make 8 triangles (32 total)
4 rectangles, 1½" × 2" (16 total)

From *each* gold print, cut:
2 squares, 1¾" × 1¾" (8 total)
2 squares, 2⅜" × 2⅜"; cut in half diagonally to make 4 triangles (16 total)
1 square, 1½" × 1½" (4 total)
7 squares, 2" × 2" (28 total)

From *one* gold print, cut:
1 square, 1½" × 1½"

From blue print #1, cut:
4 rectangles, 1½" × 4½"
14 squares, 2" × 2"

From blue print #2, cut:
14 squares, 2" × 2"

From the blue ombré, cut:
2 squares, 9" × 9"; cut in half diagonally to make 4 triangles
4 strips, 1⅛" × 21"

Assembling the Blocks

Press all seam allowances as indicated by the arrows in the illustrations.

1. Draw a diagonal line from corner to corner on the wrong side of two cream 1¾" squares. Pair a marked square with a gold 1¾" square, right sides together. Sew ¼" from each side of the line. Cut on the marked line and press. Make a total of four half-square-triangle units. Trim each unit to 1¼" square.

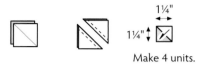

Make 4 units.

2. Sew matching cream 1⅝" triangles to the gold sides of the half-square-triangle units as shown. Make four units.

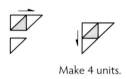

Make 4 units.

3. Sew each triangle unit from step 2 to a matching gold 2⅜" triangle. Make four units that measure 2" square.

Make 4 units,
2" × 2".

4. Arrange and sew the units from step 3 together with four matching cream 1½" × 2" rectangles and a matching gold 1½" square. The block should measure 4½" square, including seam allowances. Make a total of four blocks.

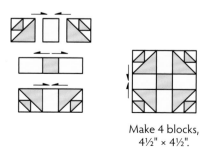

Make 4 blocks,
4½" × 4½".

Assembling the Quilt Top

1. Arrange and sew the blocks together in rows of two blocks each, along with the blue print 1½" × 4½" sashing rectangles and the remaining gold 1½" square.

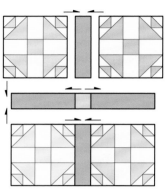

Make 1 quilt center,
9½" × 9½".

2. Sew two blue ombré triangles to opposite sides of the quilt center. Press, and then sew blue ombré triangles to the remaining sides. Trim the quilt center to measure 13½" square, including seam allowances.

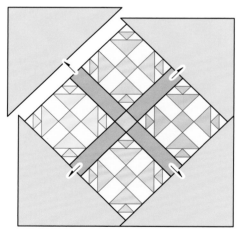

Quilt assembly;
trim to 13½" × 13½".

5. Sew the side borders to the quilt center, and then add the top and bottom borders. The quilt top should measure 15½" square.

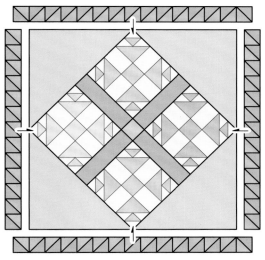

Adding borders

Finishing

For detailed information about any finishing steps, visit ShopMartingale.com/HowtoQuilt.

1. Layer the quilt top, batting, and backing; baste the layers together.

2. Quilt as desired. The quilt shown was quilted in the ditch of the blocks and with parallel, diagonal lines in the setting triangles.

3. Trim the batting and backing even with the quilt top.

4. Using the blue ombré 1⅛" strips, make and attach single-fold binding.

3. Referring to step 1 of "Assembling the Blocks" on page 28, use the assorted gold and blue print 2" squares to make a total of 56 half-square-triangle units. Trim the units to 1½" square.

Make 56 units.

4. Sew 13 half-square-triangle units together to make a side border. Make two. Sew 15 units together; make two for the top and bottom borders.

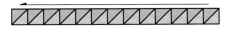

Make 2 side borders,
1½" × 13½".

Make 2 top/bottom borders,
1½" × 15½".

CHAPTER 4

Independent Women

Throughout much of our country's history, marriage was expected for most women. Many women immigrated to America as indentured servants in hopes of finding a husband as well as a new life. While being a widow at some point wasn't uncommon, being an old maid was.

Traditional roles for women were as wife and mother; keeper of the home with responsibility for food, clothing, and bedding; and nurse to the sick. Girls could attend school, but a practical needlework education at home was equally important. Children were a necessity. They would help with all aspects of farming and home life. Families provided a workforce for cities and factories.

In Puritan New England of the 1600s, women who were independent, displayed a talent, or were in any way different risked being accused of witchcraft. Conformity was the rule; individuality was not tolerated.

As settlements grew, some women became shopkeepers, innkeepers, or midwives. Other women began stepping outside the normal and expected path. They sought higher education and were active in social causes.

It helps, I think, to consider ourselves on a very long journey: the main thing is to keep to the faith, to endure, to help each other when we stumble or tire, to weep and press on.

~MARY CAROLINE RICHARDS

Old Maid's Ramble

14" BLOCK

MATERIALS

Fat eighths are 9" × 21".

2 fat eighths of different light prints
2 fat eighths of different brown prints
1 fat eighth of pink print

CUTTING

Save all leftover pieces and cut a 2½" square from each fabric to use in Journey's End (page 91).

From *one* light print, cut:
12 squares, 2¾" × 2¾"
8 squares, 2⅝" × 2⅝"; cut in half diagonally to make 16 triangles

From the pink print, cut:
8 squares, 2¾" × 2¾"

From *one* brown print, cut:
4 squares, 2¾" × 2¾"

From the *second* brown print, cut:
4 squares, 4⅜" × 4⅜"; cut in half diagonally to make 8 triangles

From the *second* light print, cut:
16 squares, 2¼" × 2¼"

ASSEMBLING THE BLOCK

Press all seam allowances as indicated by the arrows in the illustrations.

1. Draw a diagonal line from corner to corner on the wrong side of eight light 2¾" squares. Pair a marked square with a pink 2¾" square, right sides together. Sew ¼" from each side of the line. Cut on the marked line and press. Make a total of 16 half-square-triangle units. Trim each unit to 2¼" square.

Make 16 units.

2. Repeat step 1 with the remaining light 2¾" squares and the brown 2¾" squares to make eight half-square-triangle units.

Make 8 units.

3. Sew two light triangles to the brown sides of a half-square-triangle unit from step 2. Sew this pieced triangle to a brown triangle. The unit should measure 4" square. Make eight units.

Make 8 units,
4" × 4".

4. Sew two light 2¼" squares and two half-square-triangle units from step 1 together as shown. Make eight units that measure 4" square.

Make 8 units,
4" × 4".

Your Choice!

You can easily arrange your block units into either Old Maid's Ramble or Old Maid's Puzzle blocks, as they are both made up of the same components. The difference is in the orientation of the pink half-square-triangle units.

5. Arrange and sew the units together as desired to make one quarter block that measures 7½" square, including seam allowances. Two different layout options are shown below. Make four units.

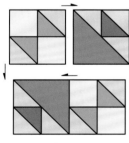

Make 4 units,
7½" × 7½".

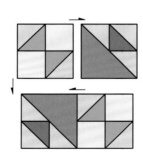

Make 4 units,
7½" × 7½".

6. Sew the quarter blocks together to make a block that measures 14½" square, including seam allowances. Two different layout options are shown below.

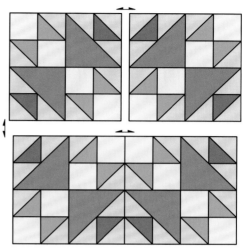

Make 1 Old Maid's Ramble block,
14½" × 14½".

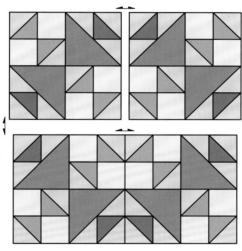

Make 1 Old Maid's Puzzle block,
14½" × 14½".

Old Maid's Puzzle or Double X

4" BLOCK

Old Maid's Puzzle

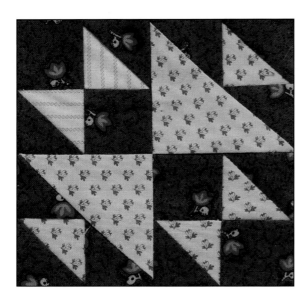

Double X

MATERIALS

1 rectangle, 6" × 10", of light stripe for background
1 rectangle, 3" × 10", of pink print for small triangles
1 rectangle, 3" × 10", of pink floral for large triangles

Note: *To reverse the values as in the Double X block, choose a dark print for the background and a light print (or two light prints) for the triangles.*

CUTTING

Save all leftover pieces and cut a 2½" square from each fabric to use in Journey's End (page 91).

From the light stripe, cut:
4 squares, 1½" × 1½"
3 squares, 2" × 2"
2 squares, 1⅞" × 1⅞"; cut in half diagonally to make 4 triangles

From the pink print, cut:
3 squares, 2" × 2"

From the pink floral, cut:
1 square, 2⅞" × 2⅞"; cut in half diagonally to make 2 triangles

ASSEMBLING THE BLOCK

Press all seam allowances as indicated by the arrows in the illustrations.

1. Draw a diagonal line from corner to corner on the wrong side of each light 2" square. Pair a marked square with a pink print 2" square, right sides together. Sew ¼" from each side of the line. Cut on the marked line and press. Make a total of six half-square-triangle units. Trim each unit to 1½" square.

Make 6 units.

Spinster

12½" × 12½" QUILT

Finished block: 1" × 1"

Despite the negative connotation of spinsterhood, many accomplished and notable women never married. Clara Barton, Louisa May Alcott, and Susan B. Anthony were just three independent, unmarried women who made enormous contributions to our history. Honor their legacy with this small quilt.

MATERIALS

Yardage is based on 42"-wide fabric; fat quarters are 18" × 21".

¼ yard of light solid for blocks
⅜ yard of red solid for blocks, border, and binding
1 fat quarter of fabric for backing
17" × 17" piece of batting
1" finished half-square-triangle paper (optional)

2. Sew two light triangles to the pink print sides of a half-square-triangle unit from step 1. Sew this unit to a pink floral triangle. The unit should measure 2½" square. Make two units.

Make 2 units,
2½" × 2½".

3. Sew two light 1½" squares and two half-square-triangle units from step 1 together as shown. Make two units that measure 2½" square.

Make 2 units,
2½" × 2½".

4. Arrange and sew the units together as shown. (Or rotate the units from step 3 to make the Double X option.) The block should measure 4½" square, including seam allowances. 🌣

Old Maid's Puzzle,
4½" × 4½".

Double X,
4½" × 4½".

CUTTING

Save all leftover pieces and cut a 2½" square from each fabric to use in Journey's End (page 91).

From the light solid, cut:
2 strips, 2" × 42"; crosscut into 32 squares, 2" × 2"*

From the red solid, cut:
2 strips, 2" × 42"; crosscut into 32 squares, 2" × 2"*
2 strips**, 2½" × 42"; crosscut into:
  • 2 strips, 2½" × 8½"
  • 2 strips, 2½" × 12½"
2 strips, 1⅛" × 42"

Or follow the cutting instructions for the triangle papers if you're using them.

**One strip may be enough, depending on the width of your fabric.*

ASSEMBLING THE BLOCKS

Press all seam allowances as indicated by the arrows in the illustrations.

Draw a diagonal line from corner to corner on the wrong side of each light 2" square. Pair a marked square with a red 2" square, right sides together. Sew ¼" from each side of the line. Cut on the marked line and press. Make a total of 64 Half-Square Triangle blocks (or use the 1" finished half-square-triangle paper). Trim each block to 1½" square.

1½"
1½"
Make 64 blocks.

ASSEMBLING THE QUILT TOP

1. Arrange and sew the blocks together in four rows of four blocks each to make a section that is one quarter of the quilt. Make four sections. Join the sections and press. The quilt center should measure 8½" square, including seam allowances.

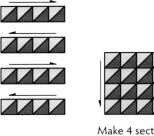

Make 4 sections,
4½" × 4½".

2. Sew the red 2½" × 8½" strips to opposite sides of the quilt top. Sew the red 2½" × 12½" strips to the top and bottom. The quilt top should measure 12½" square, including seam allowances.

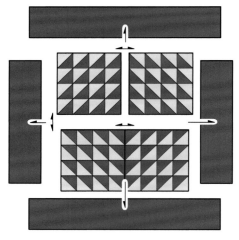

Quilt assembly

FINISHING

For detailed information about any finishing steps, visit ShopMartingale.com/HowtoQuilt.

1. Layer the quilt top, batting, and backing; baste the layers together.

2. Quilt as desired. The quilt shown was quilted with parallel diagonal lines that follow the seams and create a diamond pattern.

3. Trim the batting and backing even with the quilt top.

4. Using the red 1⅛" strips, make and attach single-fold binding. 🌸

CHAPTER 5

Captivity and Flight

Mary Draper Ingles was born in Philadelphia in 1732 to Irish immigrants. In 1748, her family moved to the western frontier of Virginia, establishing the settlement of Draper's Meadow. Mary married William Ingles in 1750. In 1755, Shawnee warriors captured Mary, who was pregnant, and two sons in the Draper's Meadow Massacre. Her husband, though badly injured, escaped.

Mary's sons were adopted by Shawnee families. After the birth of her baby, Mary was taken to Big Bone Lick, where she met an old Dutch woman who was also a captive. Together they escaped, leaving the baby behind. The two women traveled 600 miles, covering 11 to 21 miles a day with very little food. On the point of starvation, the Dutch woman tried to kill Mary for food. Mary fled, leaving the older woman behind.

Forty-two days after her escape, travelers helped Mary reunite with her husband. One son died in captivity and the other was ransomed and returned home, though he spoke only Shawnee. The baby's fate is unknown. Mary and her husband had four more children; she died in 1815 at the age of 83.

One may go a long way after one is tired.

~French Proverb

Wild Geese

6" BLOCK

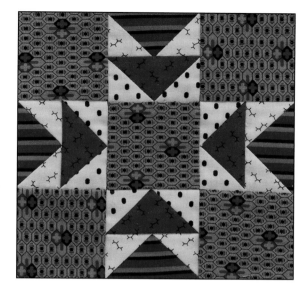

MATERIALS

2 rectangles, 5" × 8", of different light prints
3 rectangles, 6" × 10", of assorted red prints

CUTTING

Save all leftover pieces and cut a 2½" square from each fabric to use in Journey's End (page 91).

From *each* light print, cut:
4 squares, 2" × 2"; cut in half diagonally to make
    8 triangles (16 total)

From *each of 2* red prints, cut:
1 square, 3⅜" × 3⅜"; cut into quarters diagonally
    to make 4 triangles (8 total)

From the *third* red print, cut:
5 squares, 2½" × 2½"

ASSEMBLING THE BLOCK

Press all seam allowances as indicated by the arrows in the illustrations.

1. To make a flying-geese unit, sew a light 2" triangle to a red 3⅜" triangle as shown. Sew a matching light triangle to the adjacent short side. Trim the unit to 1½" × 2½", making sure that there is a ¼" seam allowance at the point of the triangle. Make four flying-geese units from each of two red prints (eight total).

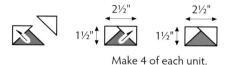

Make 4 of each unit.

2. Sew together one of each flying-geese unit to make a pair. Make four units that measure 2½" square.

Make 4 units,
2½" × 2½".

3. Arrange the four units and five red 2½" squares into rows. Sew into rows, and then sew the rows together to complete the block. It should measure 6½" square, including seam allowances.

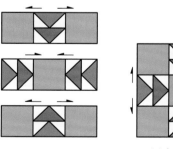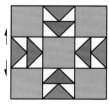

Make 1 block,
6½" × 6½".

Wild Goose Chase

4" BLOCK AND FLYING GEESE FILLER

4" Block

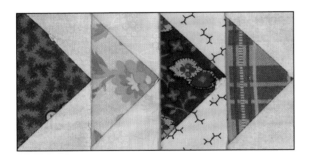

Flying Geese Filler

MATERIALS

Yardage is based on 42"-wide fabric.

⅛ yard *total* of assorted light prints
⅛ yard *total* of assorted medium to dark prints

CUTTING FOR 1 BLOCK AND 2 FILLER UNITS

Save all leftover pieces and cut a 2½" square from each fabric to use in Journey's End (page 91).

From the assorted light prints, cut:
16 squares, 2" × 2"; cut in half diagonally to make 32 triangles

From the assorted medium to dark prints, cut:
4 squares, 3⅜" × 3⅜"; cut into quarters diagonally to make 16 triangles

ASSEMBLING THE BLOCKS

Press all seam allowances as indicated by the arrows in the illustrations.

1. Sew a light 2" triangle to a medium or dark 3⅜" triangle as shown. Sew a matching light triangle to the adjacent short side. Trim the unit to 1½" × 2½", making sure that there is a ¼" seam allowance at the point of the triangle. Make 16 flying-geese units.

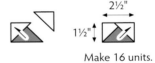

Make 16 units.

2. Sew the flying-geese units together in pairs. Make eight pairs.

Make 8 units,
2½" × 2½".

3. Join the pairs as shown to make a Wild Goose Chase block that measures 4½" square, plus two Flying Geese filler units that measure 2½" × 4½", including seam allowances. ❧

Make 1 block,
4½" × 4½".

Make 2 units,
2½" × 4½".

Rambler

10" BLOCK

MATERIALS

Fat eighths are 9" × 21".

1 fat eighth of light print
3 rectangles, 6" × 10", of assorted aqua prints
1 fat eighth of brown print

CUTTING

Save all leftover pieces and cut a 2½" square from each fabric to use in Journey's End (page 91).

From the light print, cut:
8 squares, 2¾" × 2¾"; cut in half diagonally to make 16 triangles

From *each of 2* aqua prints, cut:
1 square, 4⅞" × 4⅞"; cut into quarters diagonally to make 4 triangles (8 total)

From the *third* aqua print, cut:
2 squares, 3½" × 3½"; cut in half diagonally to make 4 triangles

From the brown print, cut:
1 square, 4" × 4"
1 square, 6½" × 6½"; cut into quarters diagonally to make 4 triangles

ASSEMBLING THE BLOCK

Press all seam allowances as indicated by the arrows in the illustrations.

1. To make a flying-geese unit, sew a light 2¾" triangle to an aqua 4⅞" triangle as shown. Sew a second light triangle to the adjacent short side. Trim the unit to 2¼" × 4", making sure that there is a ¼" seam allowance at the point of the triangle. Make four flying-geese units from each of two aqua prints (eight total).

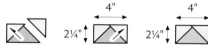

Make 4 of each unit.

2. Sew together one of each flying-geese unit to make a pair that measures 4" square. Make four pairs.

Make 4 units, 4" × 4".

3. Sew flying-geese pairs to opposite sides of the brown 4" square to make the block center. It should measure 4" × 11", including seam allowances.

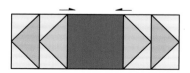

Make 1 unit, 4" × 11".

CHAPTER 7

Hope Fulfilled

*You gain strength,
courage, and confidence
by every experience in
which you really stop to
look fear in the face…
you must do the thing
you think you cannot do.*

~Eleanor Roosevelt

Ellen Gordon, a 25-year-old New York schoolteacher, married William Fletcher in 1866, just prior to embarking on their journey to Montana territory. The wagon train passed through Sioux and Crow hunting grounds on the dangerous Bozeman Trail during a relatively brief period when a peace treaty was in effect. Frequent violent attacks had been the norm as unwelcome settlers traveled through.

Ellen kept a journal that recorded many details of her trip. The newly married couple brought an abundance of supplies: 500 pounds of flour (200 pounds were recommended), canned peaches, blackberry wine, dried fruit, cod fish, bacon, ham, opera glasses, and even comfortable armchairs and two folding upholstered chairs. She felt safe and traveled in comfort, sitting in an armchair in the wagon. She was fascinated by the Native Americans and traded sugar for moccasins.

Upon their arrival in Virginia City, her husband, Billy, mined for gold and Ellen churned butter to sell. A short time later, the gold ran out. The Fletchers established a ranch and settled into their new life.

Prickly Pear

14" BLOCK

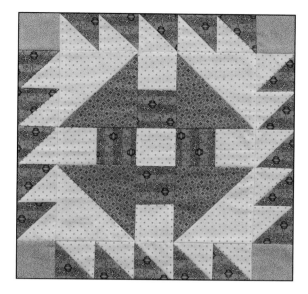

MATERIALS

Fat quarters are 18" × 21" and fat eighths are 9" × 21".

1 fat quarter of light print
2 fat eighths of different pink prints
1 fat eighth of green print
2" finished half-square-triangle paper (optional)

CUTTING

Save all leftover pieces and cut a 2½" square from each fabric to use in Journey's End (page 91).

From the light print, cut:

2 squares, 5" × 5"; cut in half diagonally to make
    4 triangles
5 squares, 2½" × 2½"
10 squares, 3" × 3"; cut in half diagonally to make
    20 triangles*

From *one* pink print, cut:

2 squares, 5" × 5"; cut in half diagonally to make
    4 triangles

From the *second* pink print, cut:

4 squares, 2½" × 2½"

From the green print, cut:

10 squares, 3" × 3"; cut in half diagonally to make
    20 triangles*
4 squares, 2½" × 2½"

Or follow the cutting instructions for the triangle papers if you are using them.

ASSEMBLING THE BLOCK

Press all seam allowances as indicated by the arrows in the illustrations.

1. Sew a light 5" triangle to a pink 5" triangle along the long edges to make a half-square-triangle unit. Trim to 4½" square. Make four units.

 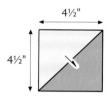

Make 4 units.

2. Sew a light 2½" square to a green 2½" square to make a unit that measures 2½" × 4½". Make four units.

Make 4 units,
2½" × 4½".

3. Arrange the units from steps 1 and 2 in three rows with the remaining light 2½" square in the middle. Sew the units into rows and then sew the rows together to make the block center. It should measure 10½" square, including seam allowances.

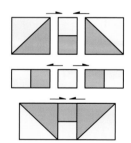

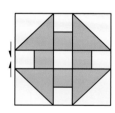

Make 1 block center, 10½" × 10½".

4. Sew a light 3" triangle to a green 3" triangle to make a half-square-triangle unit. Trim the unit to 2½" square. Make 20 units.

Make 20 units.

5. Join five half-square-triangle units into a row as shown. Make four rows. Sew a pink 2½" square to each end of two of the rows.

Make 2 rows, 2½" × 10½".

Make 2 rows, 2½" × 14½".

6. Sew the shorter rows to the sides of the block center. Sew the longer rows to the top and bottom to complete the block. The block should measure 14½" square, including seam allowances. 🧵

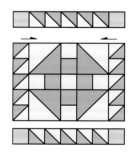

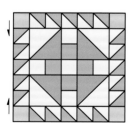

Make 1 block, 14½" × 14½".

Churn Dash

6" BLOCK

MATERIALS

1 rectangle, 8" × 10", of tan print
1 rectangle, 8" × 10", of indigo print

CUTTING

Save all leftover pieces and cut a 2½" square from each fabric to use in Journey's End (page 91). I made two of these blocks in different fabrics for my sampler quilt on page 92.

From the tan print, cut:
2 squares, 3" × 3"; cut in half diagonally to make
    4 triangles
1 square, 2½" × 2½"
4 rectangles, 1½" × 2½"

From the indigo print, cut:
2 squares, 3" × 3"; cut in half diagonally to make
    4 triangles
4 rectangles, 1½" × 2½"

ASSEMBLING THE BLOCK

Press all seam allowances as indicated by the arrows in the illustrations.

1. Sew a tan triangle to an indigo triangle to make a half-square-triangle unit. Trim to measure 2½" square. Make four units.

Make 4 units.

2. Sew a tan rectangle to an indigo rectangle as shown. Make four units that measure 2½" square.

Make 4 units,
2½" × 2½".

3. Arrange and sew the units from steps 1 and 2 into three rows with the tan 2½" square in the center as shown. Sew the rows together to complete the block. It should measure 6½" square, including seam allowances.

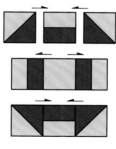 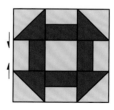

Make 1 block,
6½" × 6½".

Dashing

13¼" × 17½" QUILT

Finished block: 3" × 3"

While on the trail, cream could be put in a bucket in the morning and after a day of jostling along in the wagon, butter would be ready for the evening.

MATERIALS

Yardage is based on 42"-wide fabric.

¼ yard of yellow print for blocks

12 rectangles, 8" × 10", of assorted blue prints for blocks

6 rectangles, 9" × 12", of assorted red prints for setting blocks and triangles

⅛ yard of navy print for binding

½ yard of fabric for backing

18" × 22" piece of batting

CUTTING

Save all leftover pieces and cut a 2½" square from each fabric to use in Journey's End (page 91).

From the yellow print, cut:
2 strips, 2" × 42"; crosscut into 24 squares, 2" × 2"
2 strips, 1½" × 42"; crosscut into:
  • 48 rectangles, 1" × 1½"
  • 12 squares, 1½" × 1½"

From *each* blue print, cut:
2 squares, 2" × 2" (24 total)
4 rectangles, 1" × 1½" (48 total)

From *each* red print, cut:
1 square, 4½" × 4½"; cut into quarters diagonally to make 4 triangles (24 total)
2 squares, 3¼" × 3¼"; cut in half diagonally to make 4 triangles (24 total)

From the navy print, cut:
2 strips, 1⅛" × 42"

ASSEMBLING THE BLOCKS

Press all seam allowances as indicated by the arrows in the illustrations.

1. Draw a diagonal line from corner to corner on the wrong side of two yellow 2" squares. Pair each marked square with one of two matching blue print 2" squares, right sides together. Sew ¼" from each side of the line. Cut on the marked line and press. Make a total of four half-square-triangle units. Trim each unit to 1½" square.

Make 4 units.

2. Sew a yellow 1" × 1½" rectangle to a matching blue 1" × 1½" rectangle as shown. Make four units that measure 1½" square.

Make 4 units, 1½" × 1½".

3. Arrange and sew the units from steps 1 and 2 into three rows with a yellow 1½" square in the center as shown. Sew the rows together and press to complete the block. It should measure 3½" square, including seam allowances. Make a total of 12 blocks.

Make 12 blocks,
3½" × 3½".

ASSEMBLING THE SETTING BLOCKS AND TRIANGLES

1. To make the setting blocks, choose four assorted red 4½" triangles and sew them together in two pairs as shown. Join the pairs to make a block. Trim to 3½" square. Make a total of six setting blocks.

Make 6 blocks.

2. To make the side setting triangles, select two different red 3¼" triangles and sew them together as shown. Make a total of 10 pieced triangles.

Make 10 setting triangles.

ASSEMBLING THE QUILT TOP

1. Referring to the assembly diagram above right, arrange the blocks, setting blocks, side setting triangles, and corner triangles as shown. Sew into diagonal rows and press. Sew the rows together. Clip the intersections of the seam allowances as necessary to press toward the setting blocks and side triangles. Press the quilt top well.

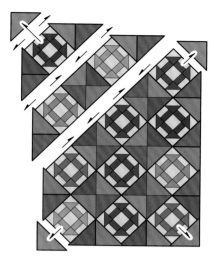

Quilt assembly

2. Trim and square up the quilt top, being sure to leave a ¼" seam allowance beyond the block points. The quilt top should measure 13¼" × 17½", including seam allowances.

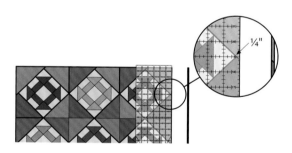

FINISHING

For detailed information about any finishing steps, visit ShopMartingale.com/HowtoQuilt.

1. Layer the quilt top, batting, and backing; baste the layers together.

2. Quilt as desired. The quilt shown was machine quilted by Karen Wood in an allover feather design.

3. Trim the batting and backing even with the quilt top.

4. Using the navy 1⅛" strips, make and attach single-fold binding. ✿

CHAPTER 8

Days of Gold

*G*old was discovered in California in 1848, kicking off a Gold Rush that lasted from 1849 to 1855.

One in every 12 miners would die in the search for gold. Deplorable living conditions, on top of the endless hours bending over to pan for gold in the streams, dashed many a miner's hope, and they often had little or nothing to show for their efforts. Most men had left families at home to seek their fortune. Some women would later head west to join their husbands, often to find the man had perished before the wife arrived. Some women braved the elements and made the transcontinental journey themselves to seek a better future.

Facing even the most dire circumstances, women survived the best they could. Some mined, some managed the gold as a bank, and some took in laundry. Others cooked for and boarded miners, and still others earned their living as prostitutes.

Quite a good living could be made as a cook, innkeeper, or laundress. As with any settlement, even primitive mining towns needed an influx of goods. Entrepreneurs saw their chance and brought shipments of merchandise to the camps, setting up stores and saloons to accommodate the ever-growing number of residents.

Were there none who were discontented with what they have, the world would never reach anything better.

~Florence Nightingale

Feathered Star

16" BLOCK

MATERIALS

Fat quarters are 18" × 21" and fat eighths are 9" × 21".

1 fat quarter of cream print
1 fat eighth of cream solid
1 fat quarter of indigo print
1 fat eighth of indigo tone on tone
1" finished half-square-triangle paper (optional)

CUTTING

Save all leftover pieces and cut a 2½" square from each fabric to use in Journey's End (page 91).

From the cream print, cut:
4 squares, 4½" × 4½"
1 square, 9¼" × 9¼"; cut into quarters diagonally to make 4 triangles
1 square, 5⅜" × 5⅜"; cut into quarters diagonally to make 4 triangles
8 squares, 2½" × 2½"

From the cream solid, cut:
12 squares, 1⅞" × 1⅞"; cut in half diagonally to make 24 triangles
12 squares, 2" × 2"*

From the indigo print, cut:
4 squares, 3" × 3"; cut in half diagonally to make 8 triangles
12 squares, 1⅞" × 1⅞"; cut in half diagonally to make 24 triangles
12 squares, 2" × 2"*

From the indigo tone on tone, cut:
4 squares, 2⅞" × 2⅞"; cut in half diagonally to make 8 triangles
1 square, 4½" × 4½"

Or follow the cutting instructions for the triangle papers if you are using them.

ASSEMBLING THE BLOCK

Press all seam allowances as indicated by the arrows in the illustrations.

1. Draw a diagonal line from corner to corner on the wrong side of four cream print 2½" squares. Place a marked square on one corner of the indigo tone-on-tone 4½" square, right sides together. Sew on the marked line, trim the seam allowance to ¼", and press. Repeat on each corner to make the star center. The star center should measure 4½" square.

Make 1 unit, 4½" × 4½".

2. Sew two indigo print 3" triangles to a cream print 5⅜" triangle to make a flying-geese unit. Trim the unit to 2½" × 4½". Make four units.

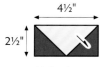

Make 4 units.

3. Sew the units from steps 1 and 2 together with the remaining cream print 2½" squares as shown to make the center star. The star should measure 8½" square, including seam allowances.

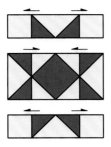 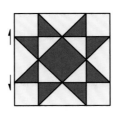

Make 1 block,
8½" × 8½".

4. Draw a diagonal line from corner to corner on the wrong side of each cream solid 2" square. Pair a marked square with an indigo print 2" square, right sides together. Sew ¼" from each side of the line. Cut on the marked line and press. Make a total of 24 half-square-triangle units. Trim each unit to 1½" square.

Make 24 units.

5. Sew three half-square-triangle units together with an indigo print 1⅞" triangle as shown. Make four of each unit.

Make 4 of each.

6. Sew two indigo print 1⅞" triangles and three cream solid 1⅞" triangles together as shown. Make eight units.

Make 8 units.

7. Sew a step 6 unit to the long side of an indigo tone-on-tone 2⅞" triangle. Then add a step 5 unit as shown to make a feathered star-point unit. Make four of each unit.

Make 4.

Make 4.

8. Sew the feathered star points to the short sides of a cream print 9¼" triangle as shown. Make four units that measure 4½" × 8½".

Make 4 units.

9. Arrange and sew the feathered star-point units together in rows with the center star and the cream print 4½" squares as shown. Sew the rows together to complete the block. It should measure 16½" square, including seam allowances. ✄

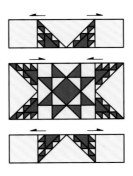 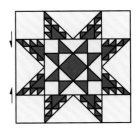

Make 1 block,
16½" × 16½".

Sawtooth Star

6" BLOCK

MATERIALS

1 rectangle, 8" × 10", of brown print
1 rectangle, 8" × 10", of cream print
1 rectangle, 4" × 7", of brown plaid

CUTTING

Save all leftover pieces and cut a 2½" square from each fabric to use in Journey's End (page 91). I made two of these blocks in different fabrics for my sampler quilt on page 92.

From the brown print, cut:
4 squares, 2½" × 2½"; cut in half diagonally to make 8 triangles

From the cream print, cut:
4 squares, 2" × 2"
1 square, 4⅜" × 4⅜"; cut into quarters diagonally to make 4 triangles

From the brown plaid, cut:
1 square, 3½" × 3½"

ASSEMBLING THE BLOCK

Press all seam allowances as indicated by the arrows in the illustrations.

1. Sew two brown print triangles to a cream triangle to make a star-point unit. Make four units and trim to 2" × 3½".

Make 4 units.

2. Arrange and sew the star-point units in rows with the cream 2" squares and the brown plaid 3½" square as shown. Sew the rows together. The block should measure 6½" square, including seam allowances. ✂

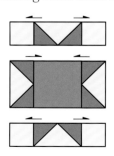
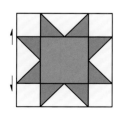

Make 1 block, 6½" × 6½".

Nugget

18½" × 12½" QUILT

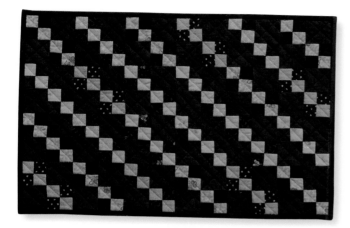

Finished block: 3" × 3"

Nugget is a simple little quilt designed to symbolize the discovery of gold and the subsequent Gold Rush in California.

MATERIALS

Yardage is based on 42"-wide fabric; fat eighths are 9" × 21".

4 fat eighths of assorted indigo prints for blocks
6 fat eighths of assorted cheddar prints for blocks
⅛ yard of indigo print for binding
½ yard of fabric for backing
17" × 23" piece of batting

CUTTING

Save all leftover pieces and cut a 2½" square from each fabric to use in Journey's End (page 91).

From *each* indigo print fat eighth, cut:
24 squares, 1¼" × 1¼" (96 total)
12 squares, 2" × 2" (48 total)

From *each* cheddar print fat eighth, cut:
16 squares, 1¼" × 1¼" (96 total)

From the indigo print for binding, cut:
2 strips, 1⅛" × 42"

ASSEMBLING THE BLOCKS

Press all seam allowances as indicated by the arrows in the illustrations.

1. Arrange and sew together two indigo 1¼" squares and two cheddar 1¼" squares as shown to make a four-patch unit. The unit should measure 2" square, including seam allowances. Make 48 units.

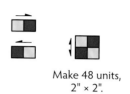

Make 48 units,
2" × 2".

2. Sew two four-patch units together with two indigo 2" squares to make a Double Four Patch block that measures 3½" square, including seam allowances. Make 24 blocks.

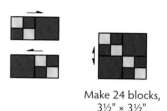

Make 24 blocks,
3½" × 3½".

ASSEMBLING THE QUILT TOP

Arrange the blocks into four rows of six blocks each. Sew the blocks into rows and then sew the rows together. The quilt top should measure 18½" × 12½", including seam allowances.

FINISHING

For detailed information about any finishing steps, visit ShopMartingale.com/HowtoQuilt.

1. Layer the quilt top, batting, and backing; baste the layers together.

2. Quilt as desired. The quilt shown was quilted in a diagonal grid.

3. Trim the batting and backing even with the quilt top.

4. Using the indigo 1⅛" strips, make and attach single-fold binding. ✤

CHAPTER 9

Life on the Trail

Luck is not chance—
It's toil—
Fortune's expensive smile
Is earned.

~EMILY DICKINSON

*O*n the wagon train, the conveniences of home became distant memories. As soon as the wagons stopped for the night, women started fires to cook the evening meal of fresh game, if lucky, or dried meats packed for the journey. Water was hard to come by, so dishes were washed with sand. After dinner, there was mending, or washing if possible, and preparations for breakfast. Women rose early and went to bed late. There was hardly time to stop for a birth or a death. There was no time to grieve and Sunday was just another day; the wagon train had to keep moving.

Wheel of Fortune

12" BLOCK

MATERIALS

Fat quarters are 18" × 21" and fat eighths are 9" × 21".

1 fat quarter of cream print
1 square, 10" × 10", of pink print
1 fat eighth of red plaid

CUTTING

Save all leftover pieces and cut a 2½" square from each fabric to use in Journey's End (page 91).

From the cream print, cut:
4 squares, 2" × 2"
8 rectangles, 2" × 3½"
2 squares, 4½" × 4½"; cut into quarters diagonally to make 8 triangles
4 squares, 3½" × 3½"

From the pink print, cut:
1 square, 6½" × 6½"

From the red plaid, cut:
8 squares, 2" × 2"
2 squares, 4½" × 4½"; cut into quarters diagonally to make 8 triangles

ASSEMBLING THE BLOCK

Press all seam allowances as indicated by the arrows in the illustrations.

1. Draw a diagonal line from corner to corner on the wrong side of each cream 2" square. Align a marked square on one corner of the pink 6½" square, right sides together. Sew on the drawn line, trim the seam allowance to ¼", and press. Repeat on each corner.

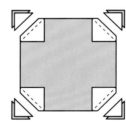 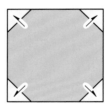

Make 1 unit,
6½" × 6½".

2. Draw a diagonal line from corner to corner on the wrong side of each red 2" square. Align a marked square on a cream 2" × 3½" rectangle. Sew on the drawn line, trim, and press as in step 1. Make four of each unit.

Make 4 of each unit,
2" × 3½".

3. Sew two cream triangles and two red triangles together into pairs as shown, and then join the pairs to make a star-point unit. Clip the intersection at the center for easier pressing. Make four units. Trim to 3½" square.

Make 4 units.

4. Arrange and sew the units and cream 3½" squares in three rows as shown. Join the rows to complete the block. It should measure 12½" square, including seam allowances. ⚜

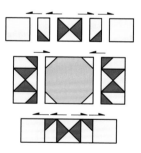 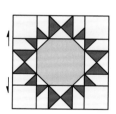

Make 1 block,
12½" × 12½".

Basket

8" BLOCK

MATERIALS

Fat eighths are 9" × 21".

1 fat eighth of cream print
1 rectangle, 5" × 10", of indigo print
1 square, 10" × 10", of brown print

CUTTING

Save all leftover pieces and cut a 2½" square from each fabric to use in Journey's End (page 91).

From the cream print, cut:
4 squares, 2¼" × 2¼"
1 square, 6" × 6"; cut in half diagonally to make
    2 triangles (1 is extra)
1 square, 4½" × 4½"; cut in half diagonally to make
    2 triangles (1 is extra)
1 square, 1¾" × 1¾"
2 rectangles, 2¼" × 5"

From the indigo print, cut:
4 squares, 2¼" × 2¼"

From the brown print, cut:
1 square, 6" × 6"; cut in half diagonally to make
    2 triangles (1 is extra)
1 square, 2⅝" × 2⅝"; cut in half diagonally to make
    2 triangles

Assembling the Block

Press all seam allowances as indicated by the arrows in the illustrations.

1. Draw a diagonal line from corner to corner on the wrong side of each cream 2¼" square. Pair a marked square with an indigo 2¼" square, right sides together. Sew ¼" from each side of the line. Cut on the marked line and press. Make a total of eight half-square-triangle units. Trim each unit to 1¾" square.

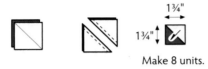

1¾"

1¾"

Make 8 units.

2. Sew the half-square-triangle units together in two rows of four as shown. Press.

Make 1 of each unit,
1¾" × 5½".

3. Sew a cream 6" triangle and a brown 6" triangle together. Press and trim to 5½" square.

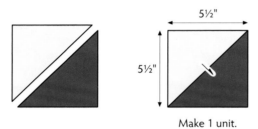

5½"

5½"

Make 1 unit.

4. Arrange and sew together the units from steps 2 and 3 with the cream 1¾" square as shown.

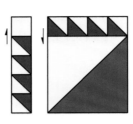 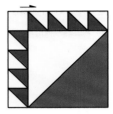

Make 1 unit,
6¾" × 6¾".

5. Sew a brown 2⅝" triangle to each cream 2¼" × 5" rectangle as shown.

Make 1 of each.

6. Sew the units from step 5 to the unit from step 4. Add a cream 4½" triangle to the remaining corner. Trim the block to 8½" square, including seam allowances. ❦

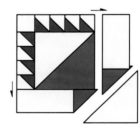 

Make 1 block,
8½" × 8½".

Cake Stand

4" BLOCK

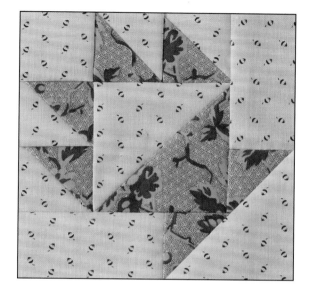

MATERIALS

Fat eighths are 9" × 21".

1 fat eighth of cream print
1 fat eighth of brown print

CUTTING

Save all leftover pieces and cut a 2½" square from each fabric to use in Journey's End (page 91). I made two of these blocks in different fabrics for my sampler quilt on page 92.

From the cream print, cut:
2 squares, 2" × 2"
1 square, 3" × 3"; cut in half diagonally to make
    2 triangles
2 rectangles, 1½" × 2½"
1 square, 1½" × 1½"

From the brown print, cut:
2 squares, 2" × 2"
1 square, 3" × 3"; cut in half diagonally to make
    2 triangles (1 is extra)
1 square, 1⅞" × 1⅞"; cut in half diagonally to make
    2 triangles

ASSEMBLING THE BLOCK

Press all seam allowances as indicated by the arrows in the illustrations.

1. Draw a diagonal line from corner to corner on the wrong side of each cream 2" square. Pair a marked square with a brown 2" square, right sides together. Sew ¼" from each side of the line. Cut on the marked line and press. Make a total of four half-square-triangle units. Trim each unit to 1½" square.

Make 4 units.

2. Sew the half-square-triangle units together in pairs as shown. Press.

Make 1 of each unit,
1½" × 2½".

3. Sew a cream 3" triangle and a brown 3" triangle together. Press and trim to 2½" square.

Make 1 unit.

4. Arrange and sew together the units from steps 2 and 3 with the cream 1½" square as shown.

Make 1 unit,
3½" × 3½".

Campfire Cake

15¾" × 15¾" QUILT

Finished block: 4" × 4"

In appreciation for help on the trail, Mary Rockwood Powers cooked the last of her dried strawberries and poured them over freshly made dumplings to serve the men who came to her aid. Cakes and pies were often made with dried fruit or berries gathered along the trail and dough of flour, water, and lard.

MATERIALS

Yardage is based on 42"-wide fabric; fat quarters are 18" × 21".

1 fat quarter of cream print for blocks

4 squares, 5" × 5", of assorted pink prints for blocks

4 rectangles, 4" × 6", of assorted brown prints for blocks

1 rectangle, 6" × 9", of cheddar print for sashing

1 fat quarter of brown stripe for border

⅛ yard of pink print for binding

⅝ yard of fabric for backing

20" × 20" piece of batting

5. Sew a brown 1⅞" triangle to each cream 1½" × 2½" rectangle as shown.

Make 1 of each.

6. Sew the units from step 5 to the unit from step 4 and press. Add the remaining cream 3" triangle to the remaining corner. Trim the block to 4½" square, including seam allowances. ✿

Make 1 block,
4½" × 4½".

Cutting

Save all leftover pieces and cut a 2½" square from each fabric to use in Journey's End (page 91).

From the cream print, cut:
8 squares, 2" × 2"
4 squares, 3" × 3"; cut in half diagonally to make
    8 triangles
8 rectangles, 1½" × 2½"
4 squares, 1½" × 1½"

From *each* pink print rectangle, cut:
2 squares, 2" × 2" (8 total)

From *each* brown print rectangle, cut:
1 square, 3" × 3"; cut in half diagonally to make
    2 triangles (8 total; 1 of each print is extra)
1 square, 1⅞" × 1⅞"; cut in half diagonally to make
    2 triangles (8 total)

From the cheddar print, cut:
4 rectangles, 1¾" × 4"

From the brown stripe, cut:
1 square, 1¾" × 1¾"
2 strips, 3½" × 9¾"
2 strips, 3½" × 15¾"

From the pink print for binding, cut:
2 strips, 1⅛" × 42"

Assembling the Blocks

Follow steps 1–6 for the Cake Stand block on page 69, using pink 2" squares for the small half-square-triangle units. Make a total of four blocks that measure 4½" square, including seam allowances.

Make 4 blocks,
4½" × 4½".

Assembling the Quilt Top

Press all seam allowances as indicated by the arrows in the illustrations.

1. Arrange the blocks with the cheddar sashing rectangles and the brown 1¾" square as shown in the assembly diagram below. Sew the pieces into rows, and then sew the rows together. The quilt center should measure 9¾" square, including seam allowances.

2. Sew the brown 3½" × 9¾" strips to the top and bottom of the quilt center. Sew the brown 3½" × 15¾" strips to the sides. The quilt top should measure 15¾" square, including seam allowances.

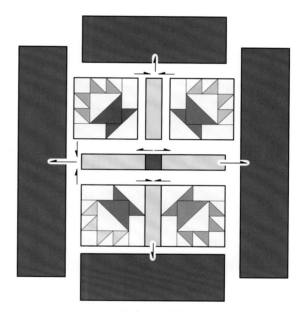

Quilt assembly

Finishing

For detailed information about any finishing steps, visit ShopMartingale.com/HowtoQuilt.

1. Layer the quilt top, batting, and backing; baste the layers together.

2. Quilt as desired. The quilt shown was quilted in the ditch of the blocks and parallel to some of the seams.

3. Trim the batting and backing even with the quilt top.

4. Using the pink print 1⅛" strips, make and attach single-fold binding. ✿

CHAPTER 10

Peace and Perseverance

After the Civil War, surviving soldiers returned home to a harsh new reality. In the South, homes were destroyed by the ravages of battle or in poor condition from neglect in a war-torn, devastated economy.

In both the North and South, jobs were hard to find. Freed slaves who went north joined an already crowded workforce. Former slaves who stayed in the South struggled to find a place to call their own, or any means to live. Many women were widowed with no support for their children or themselves. Many children were left without parents and sent to orphanages. Plantation owners, farmers, and sharecroppers in the South had no money to start over.

As a result of so many hardships, the numbers of emigrants going west increased. Whether they left crowded cities and tenement buildings or poor soil and run-down homes and farms, people went west for a fresh start, with land, job opportunities, and a future. Whole families, or women and children traveling alone, all sought a place to live and make a life. Once again, hope sustained the women as they moved into their new future.

Let me tell you the secret that has led me to my goal. My strength lies solely in my tenacity.

~LOUIS PASTEUR

Dove at the Crossroads

10" BLOCK

MATERIALS

Fat eighths are 9" × 21".

1 fat eighth of red print
1 fat eighth of brown print
1 fat eighth of cream print
1 fat eighth of indigo stripe

CUTTING

Save all leftover pieces and cut a 2½" square from each fabric to use in Journey's End (page 91).

From the red print, cut:
2 squares, 3¾" × 3¾"
8 squares, 2⅜" × 2⅜"
1 square, 2¼" × 2¼"

From the brown print, cut:
2 squares, 3¾" × 3¾"

From the cream print, cut:
4 squares, 1⅞" × 1⅞"
2 squares, 4⅛" × 4⅛"

From the indigo stripe, cut:
4 rectangles, 2¼" × 4⅝"

ASSEMBLING THE BLOCK

Press all seam allowances as indicated by the arrows in the illustrations.

1. Draw a diagonal line from corner to corner on the wrong side of each red 3¾" square. Pair a marked square with a brown 3¾" square, right sides together. Sew ¼" from each side of the line. Cut on the marked line and press. Make a total of four half-square-triangle units. Trim each unit to 3¼" square.

Make 4 units.

2. Draw a diagonal line from corner to corner on the wrong side of each red 2⅜" square. Layer two marked squares on a cream 4⅛" square as shown. The marked lines should align, and the corners will overlap. Sew ¼" from each side of the lines. Cut on the drawn line and press to make two units.

3. Layer a marked red square on the cream corner of each unit as shown. Sew ¼" from each side of the drawn lines. Cut apart and press to make four matching flying-geese units. Trim the units to 1⅞" × 3¼". Repeat to make a total of eight flying-geese units.

Make 8 units.

4. Arrange two units from step 3, one unit from step 1, and a cream 1⅞" square as shown. Sew together in rows, and then sew the rows together to make a unit that measures 4⅝" square. Make four units.

Make 4 units,
4⅝" × 4⅝".

5. Join the units with the four indigo 2¼" × 4⅝" rectangles and the red 2¼" square as shown to complete the block. It should measure 10½" square, including seam allowances. ✕

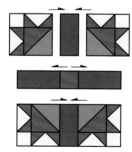 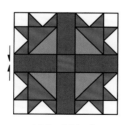

Make 1 block,
10½" × 10½".

Double T

6" BLOCK

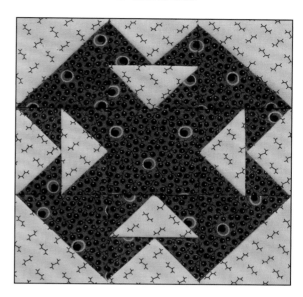

MATERIALS
1 rectangle, 8" × 12", of light print
1 rectangle, 8" × 12", of red print

CUTTING
Save all leftover pieces and cut a 2½" square from each fabric to use in Journey's End (page 91). I made two of these blocks in different fabrics for my sampler quilt on page 92.

From the light print, cut:
2 squares, 3⅜" × 3⅜"
2 squares, 3" × 3"; cut in half diagonally to make
    4 triangles

From the red print, cut:
2 squares, 3" × 3"; cut in half diagonally to make
    4 triangles
1 square, 2½" × 2½"
8 squares, 2" × 2"

ASSEMBLING THE BLOCK

Press all seam allowances as indicated by the arrows in the illustrations.

1. Sew a light 3" triangle to a red 3" triangle to make a half-square-triangle unit. Make four units and trim each unit to 2½" square.

Make 4 units.

2. Follow steps 2 and 3 of Dove at the Crossroads on page 74 to make flying-geese units with the light 3⅜" squares and red 2" squares. Make eight units and trim each to measure 1½" × 2½".

Make 8 units.

3. Sew the flying-geese units together in pairs. Make four units.

Make 4 units, 2½" × 2½".

4. Arrange and sew the units in rows as shown, adding the red 2½" square in the center. Sew the rows together to complete the block. Clip at the intersections to press the block flat. The block should measure 6½" square, including seam allowances. ✕

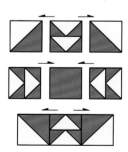
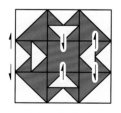

Make 1 block, 6½" × 6½".

Tenacity

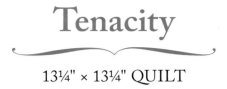

13¼" × 13¼" QUILT

Finished block: 3" × 3"

I like to think Double T stands for tenacity. This mini-quilt is for tenacious women who braved all odds during their journey across the country—across streams and deserts, plains and mountains, and lush prairies and valleys.

MATERIALS

Yardage is based on 42"-wide fabric; fat quarters are 18" × 21" and fat eighths are 9" × 21".

4 rectangles, 6" × 8", of assorted light prints for blocks

4 rectangles, 5" × 10", of assorted red prints for blocks

1 fat eighth of light brown print for setting blocks

1 fat eighth of medium brown print for setting blocks

1 fat eighth of dark brown print for setting triangles

⅛ yard of red print for binding

1 fat quarter of fabric for backing

18" × 18" piece of batting

CUTTING

Save all leftover pieces and cut a 2½" square from each fabric to use in Journey's End (page 91).

From *each* light print, cut:
2 squares, 2" × 2" (8 total)
2 squares, 2⅜" × 2⅜" (8 total)

From *each* red print, cut:
2 squares, 2" × 2" (8 total)
9 squares, 1½" × 1½" (36 total)

From the light brown print, cut:
1 square, 4½" × 4½"; cut into quarters diagonally
    to make 4 triangles
4 squares, 4" × 4"; cut in half diagonally to make
    8 triangles

From the medium brown print, cut:
1 square, 3½" × 3½"
1 square, 4½" × 4½"; cut into quarters diagonally to
    make 4 triangles
2 squares, 4" × 4"; cut in half diagonally to make
    4 triangles

From the dark brown print, cut:
2 squares, 5¾" × 5¾"; cut into quarters diagonally to
    make 8 triangles
2 squares, 3¼" × 3¼"; cut in half diagonally to make
    4 triangles

From the red print for binding, cut:
2 strips, 1⅛" × 42"

ASSEMBLING THE BLOCKS

Press all seam allowances as indicated by the arrows in the illustrations.

1. Draw a diagonal line from corner to corner on the wrong side of two light 2" squares. Pair the marked squares with matching red 2" squares, right sides together. Sew ¼" from each side of the line. Cut on the marked line and press to make a total of four half-square-triangle units. Trim each unit to 1½" square.

1½"

1½"

Make 4 units.

2. Follow steps 2 and 3 of Dove at the Crossroads on page 74 to make flying-geese units with the light 2⅜" squares and matching red 1½" squares. Make eight units and trim each to measure 1" × 1½".

1½"

1"

Make 8 units.

3. Sew the flying-geese units together in pairs to make four units that measure 1½" square.

Make 4 units,
1½" × 1½".

4. Arrange and sew the units in rows as shown, adding a red 1½" square in the center. Sew the rows together to complete the block. Clip at the intersections to press the block flat. The block should measure 3½" square, including seam allowances. Make four blocks.

Make 4 blocks,
3½" × 3½".

ASSEMBLING THE QUILT TOP

1. Sew a medium brown 4" triangle to a light brown 4" triangle to make a setting block. Trim to 3½" square. Make four blocks.

Make 4 blocks.

2. Sew a medium brown and a light brown 4½" triangle together as shown. Sew this pieced triangle to a remaining light brown 4" triangle to make a setting block. Trim to 3½" square. Make four blocks.

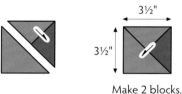

Make 2 blocks.

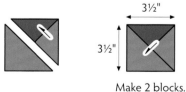

Make 2 blocks.

3. Arrange the Double T blocks, the pieced setting blocks, and the medium brown 3½" square together as shown in the assembly diagram. Add the dark brown side and corner triangles to the layout. Sew the blocks and triangles together in diagonal rows. Join the rows. Trim and square up the quilt top, leaving ¼" seam allowance beyond the block points. The quilt top should measure approximately 13¼" square, including seam allowances.

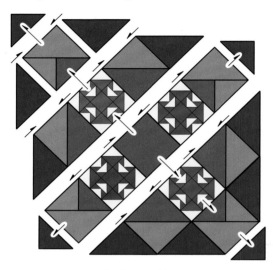

Quilt assembly

FINISHING

For detailed information about any finishing steps, visit ShopMartingale.com/HowtoQuilt.

1. Layer the quilt top, batting, and backing; baste the layers together.

2. Quilt as desired. The quilt shown was machine quilted by Karen Wood in a Baptist fan pattern.

3. Trim the batting and backing even with the quilt top.

4. Using the red 1⅛" strips, make and attach single-fold binding. ✗

CHAPTER 11

A Tale of Survival

You have to accept whatever comes and the only important thing is that you meet it with courage and with the best that you have to give.

~Eleanor Roosevelt

Olive Ann Oatman left Illinois with her family (parents and six siblings) in 1850 at age 13. The family was brutally attacked in what is now Arizona and all were killed except Olive; one sister; and one brother, Lorenzo, who was left for dead. Olive and her sister Mary Ann were taken as captives by Yavapai and became their slaves.

After a year of mistreatment, the girls were traded to the Mohave Indians, who adopted the sisters and treated them as family. The sisters were tattooed on their chins and arms, as was the tribe's custom. Olive spent four years with the Mohave before she was found and removed by the U.S. Army to be reunited with her brother. She may have left behind a Mohave husband and two children, but it was never confirmed. Mary Ann died of starvation during a famine.

A book was written about the sisters' ordeal and when Olive was speaking on the lecture circuit to promote the book, she met and married Texas cattleman John B. Fairchild. She moved to Sherman, Texas, with her husband and they adopted a baby girl.

Arrowhead Star

12" BLOCK

MATERIALS

Fat eighths are 9" × 21".

1 fat eighth of cream stripe
1 fat eighth of aqua print
1 fat eighth of brown print

CUTTING

Save all leftover pieces and cut a 2½" square from each fabric to use in Journey's End (page 91).

From the cream stripe, cut:
8 rectangles, 2" × 3½"
8 squares, 2" × 2"

From the aqua print, cut:
1 square, 3½" × 3½"
16 squares, 2" × 2"

From the brown print, cut:
8 rectangles, 2" × 5"
16 squares, 2" × 2"

ASSEMBLING THE BLOCK

Press all seam allowances as indicated by the arrows in the illustrations.

1. Draw a diagonal line from corner to corner on the wrong side of each cream 2" square and eight aqua 2" squares. Place one cream square and one aqua square on opposite ends of a brown 2" × 5" rectangle as shown, right sides together, with the light square at the top and the aqua square at the bottom. Stitch on the drawn lines. Trim the seam allowances to ¼" and press. Repeat with a second rectangle, placing the diagonal lines in the opposite direction. Make four of each unit.

Make 4 of each unit,
2" × 5".

2. Stitch the rectangles together in pairs. Make four units that measure 3½" × 5".

Make 4 units,
3½" × 5".

3. Draw a diagonal line from corner to corner on the wrong side of four brown 2" squares. Place marked squares on opposite corners of the aqua 3½" square. Stitch on the drawn lines. Trim the seam allowances to ¼" and repeat on the remaining two corners to complete the block center.

Make 1 unit,
3½" × 3½".

4. Sew two aqua and two brown 2" squares together to make a four-patch unit. Make four units that measure 3½" square.

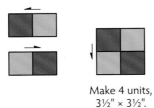

Make 4 units,
3½" × 3½".

5. Sew two cream 2" × 3½" rectangles and one brown 2" square to the four-patch unit as shown. Make four corner units that measure 5" square.

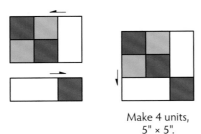

Make 4 units,
5" × 5".

6. Arrange and sew the units from step 2, the block center, and the corner units together in rows as shown. Join the rows to complete the block. It should measure 12½" square, including seam allowances. ❊

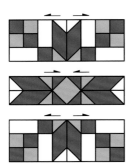 

Make 1 block,
12½" × 12½".

Postage Stamp

8" BLOCK

MATERIALS

64 squares, 1½" × 1½", of assorted prints

ASSEMBLING THE BLOCK

Press all seam allowances as indicated by the arrows in the illustrations.

1. Arrange the squares in eight rows of eight squares each in a pleasing manner.

2. Assemble the block by making a series of four-patch units. Pick up the first four squares, sew together, and replace in the layout. Press consistently in each block. "Unsew" a few stitches at the center seam intersection and flip the direction of the seams to create a little four-patch in the block center. Press all seam allowances in the same direction in each unit and they will nest together throughout the block. Make 16 four-patch units that measure 2½" square.

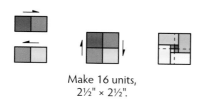

Make 16 units,
2½" × 2½".

3. Join the four-patch units into groups of four.

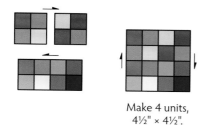

Make 4 units,
4½" × 4½".

4. Sew these units together to complete the block. The block should measure 8½" square, including seam allowances. ❋

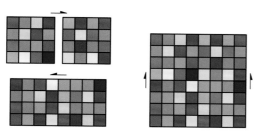

Make 1 block,
8½" × 8½".

Saw Blade

17¾" × 17¾" QUILT

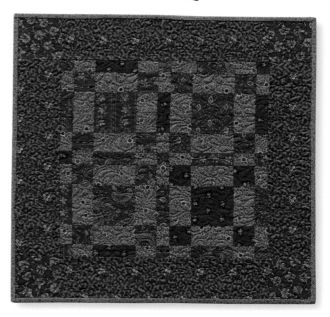

Finished block: 5" × 5

To be torn from your family twice and start over alone takes incredible fortitude. Olive Oatman's story (page 80) is a tribute to the resilience of the human spirit, and this small quilt is a tribute to her.

MATERIALS

Yardage is based on 42-wide fabric; fat quarters are 18" × 21" and fat eighths are 9" × 21".

¼ yard of aqua print for blocks and binding

1 fat eighth of light brown print for blocks and sashing

4 rectangles, 8" × 10", of assorted red prints for blocks and sashing

1 fat quarter of medium brown print for border

1 square, 10" × 10", of red print #5 for border corner squares

⅝ yard of fabric for backing

22" × 22" piece of batting

Cutting

Save all leftover pieces and cut a 2½" square from each fabric to use in Journey's End (page 91).

From the aqua print, cut:
1 strip, 2¼" × 42"; crosscut into 16 squares,
    2¼" × 2¼"
2 strips, 1⅛" × 42"

From the light brown print, cut:
16 squares, 2¼" × 2¼"
24 rectangles, 1¼" × 1¾"

From *each of 4* assorted red prints, cut:
1 square, 3" × 3" (4 total)
4 squares, 1¾" × 1¾" (16 total)
3 rectangles, 1¼" × 3" (12 total)

From the remainder of the 4 red prints, cut a *total* of:
9 squares, 1¼" × 1¼"

From the medium brown print, cut:
4 strips, 3" × 12¾"

From red print #5, cut:
4 squares, 3" × 3"

Assembling the Block

Press all seam allowances as indicated by the arrows in the illustrations.

1. Draw a diagonal line from corner to corner on the wrong side of each aqua 2¼" square. Pair a marked square with a light brown 2¼" square, right sides together. Sew ¼" from each side of the line. Cut on the marked line and press. Make a total of 32 half-square-triangle units. Trim each unit to 1¾" square.

Make 32 units.

2. Sew the half-square-triangle units into pairs measuring 1¾" × 3". Make 16 pairs.

Make 16 pairs,
1¾" × 3".

3. Arrange and sew the half-square-triangle pairs, a red 3" square, and four matching red 1¾" squares into three rows as shown. Sew the rows together to complete the block. It should measure 5½" square, including seam allowances. Make four blocks.

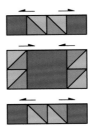 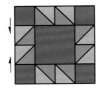

Make 4 blocks,
5½" × 5½".

Setting Three

Finished size: 48½" × 64½"

Quilt made by Sonja Kraus

Blocks Needed

- 1 block, 16½" square
- 2 blocks, 14½" square
- 6 blocks, 12½" square
- 4 blocks, 10½" square
- 2 blocks, 8½" square
- 8 blocks, 6½" square
- 4 blocks, 4½" square

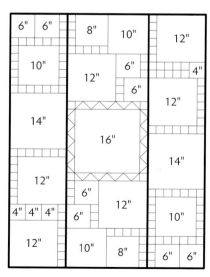

Setting 3

Setting Four

Finished size: 60½" × 60½"

Quilt made by Nancy Barton

Blocks Needed

- 1 block, 16½" square
- 2 blocks, 14½" square
- 5 blocks, 12½" square
- 4 blocks, 10½" square
- 2 blocks, 8½" square
- 12 blocks, 6½" square
- 11 blocks, 4½" square

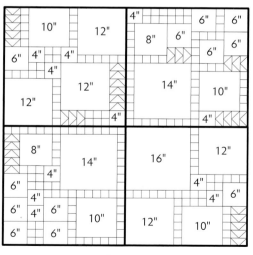

Setting 4

About the Author

Betsy developed a passion for fabric, quilts, and history as a child. After receiving a degree in history in 1980, Betsy taught herself to quilt with a quilt top made by her paternal great-grandmother and great-aunt. She began teaching quiltmaking in 1990 and continues to teach and share her passion for reproducing nineteenth-century quilts.

Betsy is a fabric designer for Moda Fabrics and the author and coauthor of several books, including *19th-Century Patchwork Divas' Treasury of Quilts* (Martingale, 2016), as well as a contributor to several compilation books featuring Moda designers.

Betsy is cofounder of the quilting group 19th-Century Patchwork Divas and lives in Grand Prairie, Texas, with her husband, Steve.

ACKNOWLEDGMENTS

It is with deep appreciation that I thank the following people:

Everyone at Martingale who worked on my book to make it so special and beautiful. Thank you for seeing my vision and for the opportunity to share my passion for quilts and women's history.

My students and club members, who blindly followed me on the mystery of Hope's Journey. Thank you for trusting me when I promised it would all go together.

Debbie Roberts, her students, and club members at the Quilted Moose in Gretna, Nebraska, for agreeing to be my test group and going on this journey with me.

Karen Wood and Maggi Honeyman, for beautiful quilting, and Renita Hall, for her help in binding the little quilts.

My friends and family, for their continuing support.

And my husband, Steve, who, years ago, in a very different context, said, "I don't know where I'm going, but follow me anyway." So many times throughout the writing of this book I've recalled your words and smiled. Thanks, Steve, for making me laugh and accompanying me on my journey.